John Hegley was born in north London and brought up in Luton. He started out as a stand-up comedian/poet, performing on the festival and comedy circuit, and soon acquired something of a cult following, becoming one of the most highly regarded British poets. More recently John has been performing his poetry for both adult and family audiences at venues across the UK.
His children's books include *My Dog Is a Carrot* and
The Adventures of Monsieur Robinet. John Hegley is a Fellow of the English Association and lives in north London.

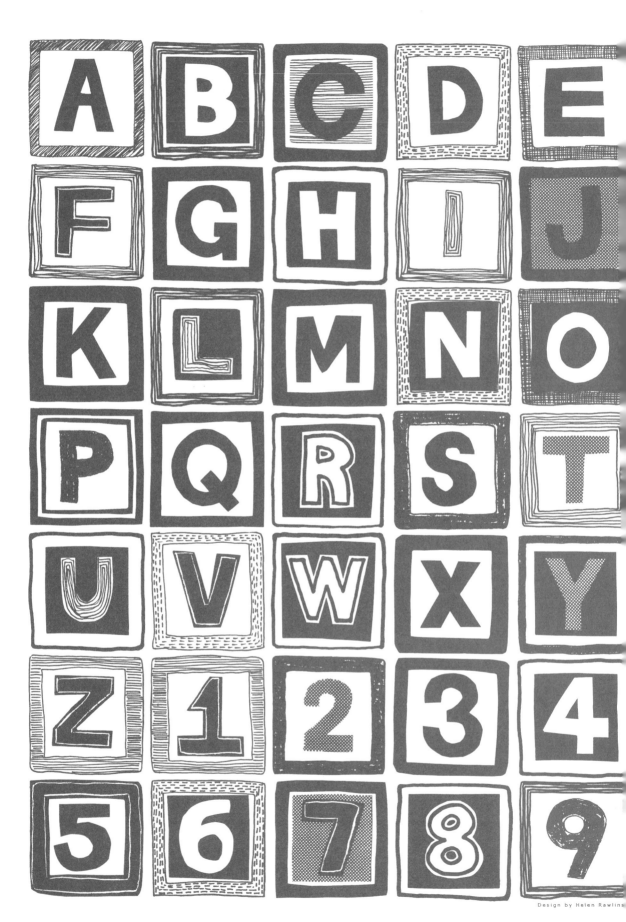

Design by Helen Rawlins

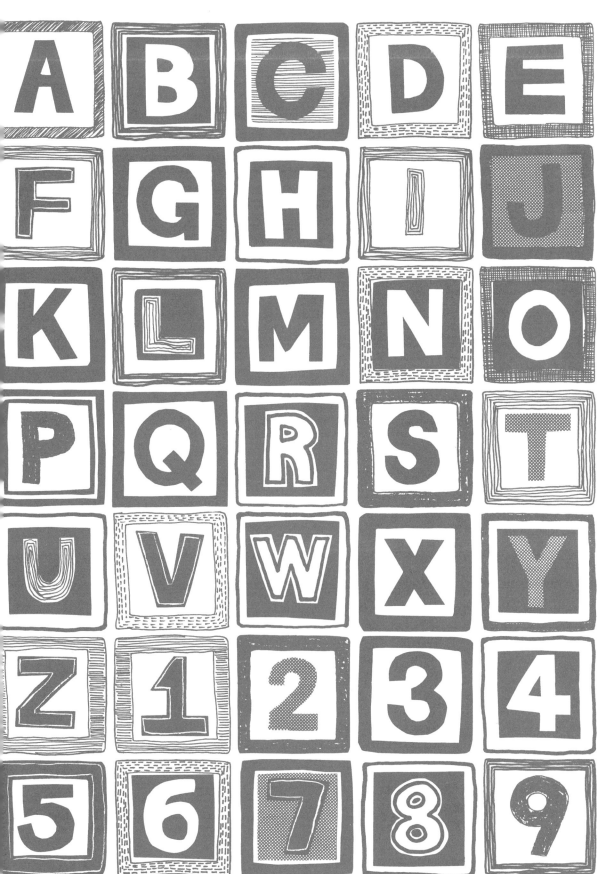

Design by Helen Rawlinson

I AM A POETATO

FOR ISABELLA

JANETTA OTTER-BARRY BOOKS

Text and illustrations copyright © John Hegley 2013
except: letters of the alphabet copyright © Helen Rawlinson 2013

First published in Great Britain in 2013 and in the USA in 2014 by
Frances Lincoln Children's Books,
74-77 White Lion Street, London N1 9PF
www.franceslincoln.com

First paperback published in Great Britain and in the USA in 2015

A catalogue record for this book is available from the British Library.

ISBN 978-1-84780-600-0

Printed in China

9 8 7 6 5 4 3 2 1

I AM A POETATO

AN A–Z OF POEMS ABOUT PEOPLE, PETS AND OTHER CREATURES

JOHN HEGLEY

Frances Lincoln
Children's Books

CONTENTS

ALLIGATOR

To an alligator, you look yum.

You are yum to the tum of an alligator.

Though you can think and you can feel,

To an alligator, you are a meal deal.

To an alligator's scrunch, you're Lunchtime.

To an alligator's eyes, you're bite-size.

You're no pal of the alligator.

But you can't get on with everyone, can you?

ANTS

In Australia.
Summer, with Isabella
four winters old, in her swimming cozzie.
I'm finding it hard to tell her stuff...
like, *'Put your shoes on when we walk*
the wooden walkway to the beach,
or you'll get splinters!'
'I won't get splinters,
I won't put my shoes on. No!'

The passing Australian woman
stops at our struggling and tells her,
'You should put your shoes on real quick.
*There are **bull ants**.'*
Quickly averse to this idea
Isabella puts on her shoes.
*'**Bull ants** – what are they?'* she wonders.
'What are they?' echoes the Aussie
with the voice of fear.
*'...They are **big**.*
*They are **poison**.*
And, they are here.'

A MOSQUITO

I whirl,
I whizz,
I'm not an ant.
I is the Moz,

I'm a flighty

BITEY,
MIGHTY
irritant.

BEES

Luton Town Football Club
have won the league
and today, in the game against Brentford, The Bees,
they will be given The Cup.
I have gone up to Luton on the train
even though I know there are no tickets left.
I just want to sit near the ground
and hear the sound of the **FANS** inside
CHEERING Luton along.

As I walk towards the stadium,
I see a man
who has been flogging flags
on sticks in the street.
He is packing away all that he has not sold.

As I go and sit by the ground
I see a pile of S T I C K S
I do not realise straight away
that they are from fans
who have bought the man's flags.

However, when I see a single flag attached
I suppose the stewards have said to the supporters,
'You can't bring the sticks inside the ground
as they might go in someone's eye.'
One purchaser has obviously decided
they can't be bothered
to detach their flag
and here it lies in the heap.

I pick it up, and sit beside the turnstiles
ready to start waving, if Luton score.

They do score, and I wave the flag W I L D L Y .
The people in the ground may be able
   to see the game,
but they can't have the same F U N as me,
   waving their flags,
because they don't have any S T I C K S .

CAT

We have a cat.
We give her dry biscuits for lunch,
and when she is at her meal
we call her **Captain Crunch.**
In my mind I can see her
in a little Super-hero's cloak
made from a facecloth
and she's bombing down with
flower-bunches
to comfort females
whose dads
refuse them affection.

CHRISTMAS CATERPILLAR

It crawled up Santa's trousers
with all its little legs
and that creepy kept on crawling
with Santa unaware
until he felt a tiny tickle
and he went ooh ooooh
oooooooh ooo ooh
ooooooooooooh

oooh

ooh

11

DIFFERENCES BETWEEN DOGS AND DECKCHAIRS

A deckchair doesn't beg

or cock up its leg.

Deckchairs don't sniff each other.

Deckchairs can't swallow,

or swim, or growl.

Deckchairs aren't HER or HIM.

Deckchairs don't join in games with sticks.

There are no prizes for WELL-TRAINED deckchairs.

Deckchairs rarely have names, except 'deckchair'.

People don't have trouble putting up a dog.
Dogs' legs don't have little notches in.
A deckchair's legs are MUCH STIFFER
with no knees.
A dog is better at running after Frisbees.
Deckchairs can be STACKED quite neatly.
Dogs have more hairs.
Deckchairs have more letters.
Deckchairs don't sniff about in Autumn leaves.
A deckchair receives little praise.

DOGS

LARGE DOG – What do you think you're getting,
the bone or the triangle?
SMALLER DOG – The triangle.
LARGE DOG – That's right.

LET SLEEPING DOGS LIE
UNLESS THEIR KENNEL IS ON FIRE.

ELEPH ANT

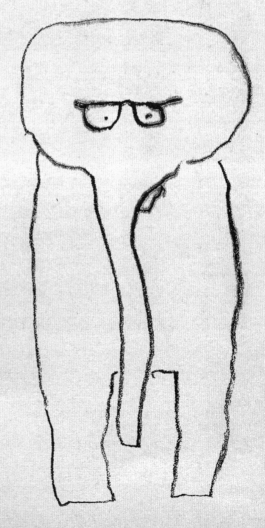

LONG trunk caller
Tusk tusk GIANT
Undergrowth CRUSHER
Big foot FATTY
Full-eared FLAPPIT.

FISHTOES

One day John
looked down and saw that his bottom bit
had gone
all fishy.

John said to Janet that he didn't know
how he was going to get his football shorts on.
Janet ~~said~~ answered that now was the time to give up football
and start swimming more.
John ~~replied~~ said that he would never fit
in the goldfish bowl.

Floating
Isn't
So
HARD

Frying
Isn't
So
HOT

For
Instance
Some
HALIBUT

GUILLEMOT

I am a guillemot

I use my bill a lot

I get the fish out of the wet

I eat my fill a lot.

I live on ledges

VERTICAL EDGES

Eating-wise, I do not know what veg is.

Don't give me sherbert

Give me a turbot

My appetite for fish, I cannot curb't,

Here's lines more

in the manner of George Herbert:

The fish, it swimmeth unaware

And rumbled, down

I tumble

towards my prey

My instincts I obey.

From WATER to the STIFLING AIR
I'll whip the little whipper-snap away
I am a guillemot
I know the drill a lot
I drill into the drink
And get the ink
And not the drink
Upon my quill a lot
So, you don't thrill a lot?
Well, *listen humans*, very soon you will a lot
Did you know that I can go so DEEP
I've been seen
From the porthole of a submerged submarine,
a hundred and thirty metres under?
I don't think so
Miss it and blink so
I come in **hard**, and I am able to sink so.

I am a guillemot

I do my perchin'
And my researchin'
Then underneath I go, I'm no sea urchin
I am a diver
Ocean-arriver
Underneath I go
I am no skiver
I am a guillemot
I find the fishes tend to lose one-nil a lot
But I take only what I need
I'm not a GREEDY bird
I am sustainable
Self-restrainable
I am a guillemot

I am homeless
But I'm not gormless

I sleep *rough.*
I've got no stuff.
But what I am will always be enough.
I am homeless, but I'm not gormless.

I can go so quick, it's almost like I'm formless
I am a guillemot

I don't do **nesting**
When I am **resting**
I can sleep while I am standing on one leg
And so it doesn't roll off
When I stretch my wings
Or stroll off
I've got an egg that is conical and eccentrically weighted
so it doesn't fall off the edge of the cliff
I am a guillemot
I don't eat Trill a lot
I do my speccy reccy from my rocky window sill a lot
I am a guillemot
      am I not.

GNAT POEM

You certainly know how to flit.
You know how to gnatter and gnit
      your invisible stitches
And I've heard that your pitch is
A colony in the same bit of woodland
For centuries, sometimes.

HAMSTAR

I'm a **hamStar**
that's what I **amStar**
small enough to fit into a jam jar.
I've got a treadmill to keep in trainin'
I've got a little head to keep my brain in
And pouches at the side
to keep my grain in.

Once our hamster
got out of its cage.
Titchy thought he was **FREE**
which he was.
But freedom brings
its own problems.
In this case it was the cat.
Luckily Titchy stood up to Ella, as fierce as a **LION**
and the cat went and ate some biscuits.

HORSIE

Isabella,
you are **9** today.
You ask me to look at the **horsie.**
I suppose it's not long now
before **horsie** takes a bow,
and the creature is spoken of
in a grown-up way.
It will become a horse,
not a **horsie,**
in due course.

Invisible Hamster

In my jacket pocket
beside my lapel
is the unseen hamster-life.

The creature is clinging
        to the pocket-top

looking out like it's a parapet.

Occasionally it dips below
        into its small packet
            of hamster treats,
which you cannot see or smell, either.

The hamster eats
            very quietly

But its nose is wet as any

And it's better at shoulder-climbing, than many.

It is my sham-hamster-king.
It is my mock-pocket-hamsterchief.

ISABELLA'S COMPLAINT

What ar you doing,

. . . putting a pare in my lunchbox?

Your mad.

Evryone els has an aple.

I don't want to be different

I don't want them to stair.

Dont you dare.

What are your thinking of?

Putting a pare

of socks

in my lunchbox?

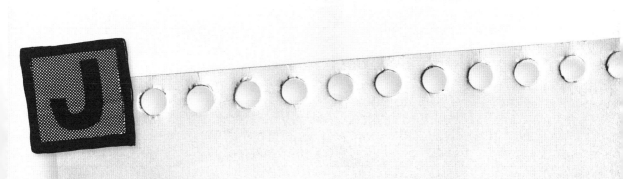

JOURNEY TO JUBILATION

Toby, the armadillo from Peru, is my small friend.
He, the dog and I, sometimes played together
by the bend in the river.
One morning I saw that Toby was not under my pillow
where he usually liked to rest.
Distressed,
and without taking time to get dressed
I hurried down to the river to look for him.
There he was, in a boat, waggy,
with next-door's dog
and I thought, even though
It hurts me to see him go
I'm glad that somebody else is making him happy.

Twenty-five years later
I rang up an Irish monastery
and asked if I could spend a little time there
for QUIET and REST.
My request was approved
and when I arrived in Galway
I did not know that Toby's new home was there.
Even when I heard next-door's dog barking
I didn't get a clue.

I thought Toby had gone back to Peru, you see.
So, when I saw him stood there in the hallway
it was just the tonic I needed.
And Toby and I *ran* and *rolled* in the hills roundabout.
And later I stickytaped some daffodils to him
and called him Armadeus the Daffodillo.

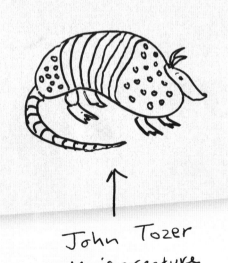

John Tozer
drew this creature

KIKI AND KOKO

When my grandma came to England from France,
she glanced at the fish and said
'What are their names?'
And my sister and I said
they didn't have any.
And our French Gran said
'It's a shame, but they can be called Kiki and Koko.'
And when she went back to Nice
these names were a little piece of France left in our home
along with the French windows,
which didn't have any names either.

MICETROES

Triangle jangler by A. Curtis.

MICYCLE

NIT NURSE

She came to school to nab the nit
Her white coat did not quite fit
She was too tall for it
And I loved her for it
Nitty Nora – The Bug Explorer
Mr Brennan's name for her was Nurse
The children's name was better
Each child's head was frisked in turn
Nora came to school to learn
Who had **nits** and who had not
I liked her **Nitty** name a lot
...she had a hand in every head
A cross between someone typing words
And someone kneading bread
She clawed and looked and looked and clawed
And made a mark upon her clipboard

She never let it slip whose barnet had been nested
and when all of us were done and tested
She left the clean and the bug infested

Nitty Nora The Bug Explorer

I don't think she'd have minded us

Referring to her thus,

She seemed a playful creature.

Our teacher, Mister Brennan, liked a verse,

He liked to play with languages.

He had to be sensible and call her Nurse,

but I'm sure he would much rather have piped up with

PLEASE WILL YOU ALL WELCOME
NITTY NORA
THE BUG EXPLORER!

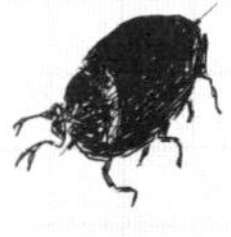

OWL POEM

On
Wards
Lofty

Oh,
Winged
Looker

Out
Witting
Low-life

Ooooh
Wooooooo
Language

OWL

There's an owl outside the window; it used to be
crossed out. But, the crossing out's been made into
a window and now the owly eyes
are looking in.

Open Wide Lids
On Window Ledge

We are drawing owls
When we are finished
I look at yours and tell you I quite like it
You cross it out.
Two angry strokes of a pen
Cross.

I say 'Why did you do that?'
You say 'Because it's rubbish.'
I say 'What are you saying? It's fantastic
look at all the detail on the head!'

I say the owl can be saved.
I make the cross into some criss-crossing windows
You join in with the new drawing.
The owl is saved
I think it best not to add
that your window ledge
needs a bit of work.

And perhaps I might have mentioned
the detail on the head
a little earlier.

PETER THE PARROT

Peter the orange parrot
had a very tiny beak,
unlike the other parrots
he was never heard to speak.

But they were never nasty to him,
Peter the non-talking parrot
they just thought that he was
a very very fluffy carrot.
Then one sunny jungle day
Santa Claus got lost
and Peter with the tiny beak
suddenly was heard to speak
and he directed Santa back to Lapland
to be in the lap of all the other lovely Lapps;
while the other parrots had been talking

Peter had been reading maps

Composed with help from Jane Ireland

POTATO

'What's this then, Joan?' said her brother Tony,
pointing to a familiar-looking object on the table.
Joan didn't understand...
'A stone!' said Joan. 'Well, what about it?'
'Hold your hand out,' said Tony, picking it up
and placing it in her palm.
Joan's fingers curled about the object.
She felt a little alarmed.
This wasn't a stone at all.
This was a POTATO.

'You can keep it if you want to,' said Tony,
'I've got loads of them.'
'Wow. Thanks,' said Joan,
'this will be my LUCKY POTATO.'
'I don't think there's such a thing as a LUCKY POTATO,'
answered Tony, pointing out how they got
chopped, sliced, boiled, roasted, mashed and eaten.
'I know all that,' said Joan, 'I mean lucky for me,
not lucky for *it*.'

PONY

Brother, I have your Pony, made of cloth.
I am eleven.
But I am not too old for this soft toy friendship.
The clothes that you grew out of,
I was often put inside.
I wore your woolly swimming trunks
and windcheater with pride.

I followed close behind your steps.
I went into the woods with you.
I went down to the DUMP with you.
I wasn't in the DUMPS with you.
It always felt so good with you,
until you decided that you needed friends of your own age
with motorbikes.
Still, I get to hold your worn-out woollen Pony at night,
now that you are too big for cuddling animals
and too big
for your small brother.

Dear Jane, today I go another way.
I leave our primary school where we have been ok.
I wish we could have been friends here.
I'd like to make amends.
I wanted to soften, but stayed **stony-eyed.**
I was too good at disguises.
When they tried to hold me down for you to kiss me
I threw them off and ran away.
I could have kicked myself that day.
Anyway before we say goodbye,
let me give you my old cloth dog and lamb.

But you can't have Pony.

QUEEN BEE

Hello Workers
I'm your Queen.
I keep myself
Extremely clean.
I give orders
You just take.
It's time for work
You've had your break
Take your yellow, take your black,
Bring the stuff for honey back
Off you go, I've eggs to lay
What I'm trying to say
is, Buzz Off.

Isabella's backward bee

40

QUIBBLE

The QUIBBLE
likes an argument
at any time of day,
morning or night.
You might hear the QUIBBLE say,
'That's not quite right, is it?
or, *'Are you sure, Barbara?'*

Roo the day

ROO THE DAY

A kanger is part of a roo.
Detectives will look for a clue.
Picasso he painted and drew.
Tourists may look for a view,
Or a monument.
The 'wow' of a cow is a Moo.
Ghosts never cheer they say **BOO.**
Take library books back when they're due.
A perch in a church is a pew.
You've left me and I'm missing you.

UNDERDOG

RUF RUF

A **RUF RUF'S** what
we call a dog
we don't call a cat a
MEOW MEOW
but we do say
QUACK QUACK
sometimes
and we do
say
MOO COW – half noise, half naming.

SNAKE

Sneaker.
Always lying low.
Hosepipe.
Where does neck end
And back begin?
No arms or legs.
Have you
got any
ears?
Snake,
you make
me think
and wonder.
Slider,
Slipper.

Curving
Swerving,
Egg-layer.
Some people
have you
as a pet,
and yet,
they know
you will never
chase a ball
a stick
or a Frisbee.
Snake
you say
tHISS
and you say
it all day
long.

SNAIL POEM

The snail leaves a tell-tale trail
   shining like a railway rail.On its back is quite a pac
a castle and a gaol. The snail's house is not for sale,
request for speed to no avil. SLOW SLOW no quick, just slow.

                                    avail

SNAIL

TORTOISE

JOHN: If you let me come round to your house you can borrow my pet tortoise.

JANET: My mum doesn't like me borrowing.

JOHN: Ok, you can have it... you can have it for a week.

JANET: Why would I want to have it though?

JOHN: Because a tortoise has got a **primordial** look about it.

JANET: What does that mean?

JOHN: It means it looks even OLDER than my dad. You get a sense of your links with the ice age with a tortoise.

JANET: But I've already got a pet hamster.

JOHN: A tortoise is **better** than a hamster.

JANET: But a tortoise doesn't have food pouches in its jowls.

JOHN: No, but it's got a really **HARD** shell and it's **HARD** to spell as well. It looks like it should rhyme with noise, but it doesn't want to, and so it doesn't. *End of story.*

JANET: Please, don't say that phrase.

JOHN: What phrase?

JANET: *End of story.* It's irritating and it's not the end of the story, either. Can a tortoise run around in a wheel?

JOHN: My tortoise doesn't run, even. It takes its time. It does what it wants.

JANET: What about if it wants to escape?

JOHN: It escapes very slowly. It's great, and you can have it for a week, if you let me come round to your house.

JANET: What for?

JOHN: So I can see your hamster.

TIBBY CAT

Our first burst of petness
was Tabby cat, Tibby.
In the Runfold area of Luton.
A **TOUGH COOKIE** cat.
A **WILD** thing.
The scrawny riverbank nearby was just his ticket.
The day we were deserting the house to go
and take up residence in the bungalow
that cat didn't want to know.

My dad approaching with a sack.
The back of the removal van tightly-packed,
but still with S P A C E for one more item,
and Tibby ran
in Runfold.
Tibby wouldn't go.
We'd not see one more Tibby paw-print
pressed in Luton snow.

Cat shading by J. Sleeman.

Unicorn and friend
by Faye Hobson

UNUSUAL UNICORN IN THE SCHOOL

We keep it in the corner of the playground.

It poked me with its horn only this morning.

Why can't we have a school pet that is **NORMAL?**

Why have we got to have a cross

between a **HORSIE** and a RHINO?

Excuse my *scorn*

But I don't like our school *unicorn.*

VOLE IN A VEST

On Tuesday night, I couldn't rest.
I was down, and right depressed,
I felt as though I wasn't blessed.
A little pest
was bothering me,
I was down.
And down the stairs I went,
to get some string out of
the kitchen drawer
to make myself a vest.
A vest of string – as just a lad
I saw a string vest on my dad
and he seemed glad enough.
Like other stuff to wear we had,
it had some holes in
but not so many voles in.

None in fact,
and if there had been any
my mother would have seen them off.
Maybe they'd have hidden in the socks
she used to darn.
I'll be darn honest with you
whoever you are
I'm not sure what a vole looks like
but I just know my mum would have seen them
right off
however big
however ignominious.

WISE CAMEL

I'm the **BEAST**
that bore
wise man number four
We're the ones who went North
when the others went West
We followed, not the Star of David
but the star of Steve.
My rider wasn't sure that his gift
was as good as the other three.
I sometimes wonder
if we got lost on purpose.
Myself, I thought
he brought the best gifts, actually:
the gift of straw,
the gift of warmth.

Warmth for the manger
But because he wasn't sure
his gift was good enough
he kept adding
straw after straw
It was the last one that did it.
So I'm on the wrong track
with a **BUSTED** back
but luckily we found this town
with a really good vet.
And, in the end,
had a **PLEASANT,**
if **RATHER QUIET,** Christmas.

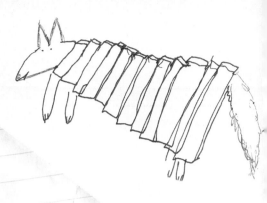

XYLOFOX

a fox of thoughts
a box of tricks
it can't be caught
or played with sticks
the xylo, furry
cunning fox
it don't wear shoes
it don't wear out
its socks or gloves
it loves its den
it's cheated death
it don't eat chicken
it's got some very tuneful mates
it eats its words off armour plates.

XYLOMICE

by Isabella

YARD BIRD

Bird was a nick-name
of Charlie Parker,
an American saxophone parper
who played a style of Jazz music, called Bebop.

But not *knobbly-knee-bop.*

When I first heard Bird,
I did not understand his music.
But when I listened some more, I liked it.
Sometimes poetry is like that.
You need more than one go at it.
Bird got sickly and died very young,
because he did not look after himself properly.
They say an apple a day keeps the doctor away.
Well, I don't know how many apples Bird ate,
But he did make up a tune called
Scrapple from the Apple.

But not *Scrorange from the Orange,*
Scrackberry from the Blackberry
or *Scrapefruit from the Banana.*

YOUCAN

The hoover needed mending.
I said, *'it's not the sort of thing I do, is it,'*
But I removed the muck and put the suck
back in that hoover
the day the Youcan came to visit.

The Youcan is a bird which helps the difficult get done.
The sound it makes is *'Doo-it'.*

One day I wouldn't say, *'I'm sorry,'*
I felt I was too **TOUGH**
but when the Youcan flew
I wasn't able to
APOLOGISE enough.

I thought I'd never hula-hoop
I said, *'I haven't got the knack.'*
But then the Youcan swooped
and I hula-hooped.
And I really hurt my back.

ZEBRA

She's a spotty zebra:
a zebra, without a single stripe,
a zebra of a different type.
The other zebras don't mind
this zebra of a different kind,
they seem, in fact, to approve.
They certainly don't take any steps
to hasten her removal.
Zebra is a stripy word,
but still, she hangs about the herd
from March to Febra.

What is a spot, anyway?
A stripe curled up in a ball?
Or one that's very short
with rounded ends?
Whatever it is, she descends
to splosh about in water holes
with her friends
and they wash and nosh
as though she's one of them,
the zebra, the spotty zebra.
Where can you see her?
Is it on the wide Savannah
or is it inside the Safari park
near Kidderminster in Bewdley?
I don't know.

All I know is that the other Zebbos
never treat her rewdley,
and they don't get stroppy with her;
they like her not copying the norm.
She's got her own individual form.
The spotty zebra's a hit
with the more conventional zebras.
The stripy donkey however,
doesn't have such an easy time of it.

Spotty zebra by Ivan Bailey Wilson

ZOMBIE

That man... he's walking like he's turned into a Zombie.
I wonder who he is and where he's frombie?
I wonder if his boiler is a Combi?
I wonder if he'd be glad if I asked him if he needs any help?

ZOË

Zoë Zoë
You had to goë
I felt so sad,
I wrote this poë.

The dog runs

Not after the nuns,

after the buns

or are they potatoes?

who knows?

The cat

knows

Nothing

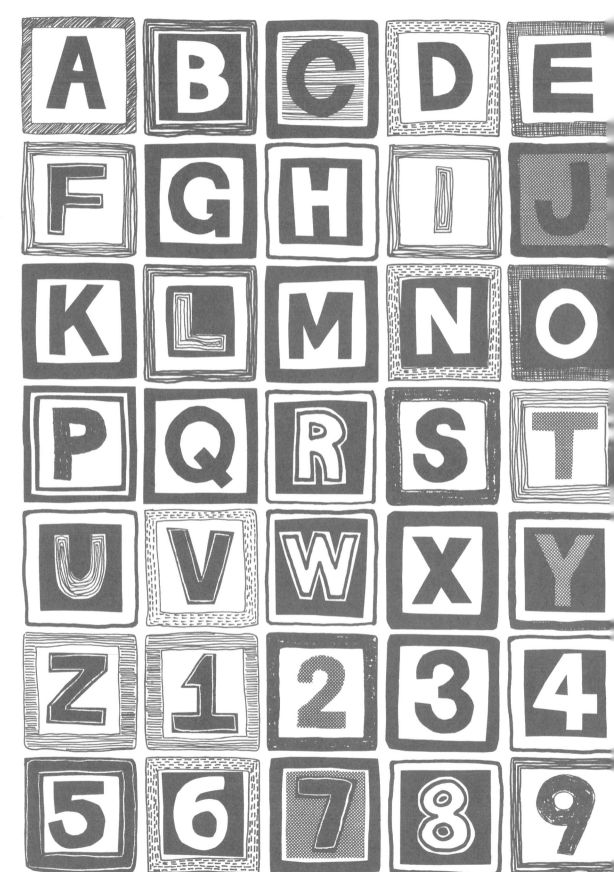

Design by Helen Rawlins

Design by Helen Rawlinson

MORE GREAT POETRY PUBLISHED BY FRANCES LINCOLN CHILDREN'S BOOKS

An Imaginary Menagerie
Roger McGough

A witty and wicked collection of poems with illustrations by the author, featuring an amazing A-Z of animals real and imaginary.

"Classic Roger McGough... Kids love these poems." – *The Guardian*

"Fun, clever, fun!" – *School Librarian*

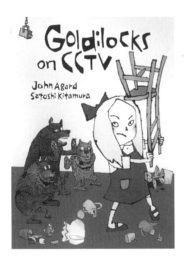

Goldilocks on CCTV
John Agard

Poor Goldilocks, caught on camera breaking into a house of suburban grizzlies...

"A lyrical feast, starring a busted Goldilocks, a biker Cinderella and Puss-in-Trainers" – *English 4-11*

Frances Lincoln titles are available from all good bookshops.
You can also buy books and find out more about your favourite titles,
authors and illustrators on our website: www.franceslincoln.com